What's Your Make Up?

A 30-Day Makeover Journey

to Discover Your Godly Make Up

BY HANNAH GREER
2019

Never forget — you are God's beautiful and valuable daughter!

Hannah Greer

COVER DESIGN BY ERYNNE JAMISON
2019

Scripture quotations marked ESV have been taken from the ESV® Bible (The Holy Bible, English Standard Version®), copyright © 2001 by Crossway, a publishing ministry of Good News Publishers. Used by permission. All rights reserved.

Scripture quotations marked HCSB have been taken from the Holman Christian Standard Bible®, Copyright © 1999, 2000, 2002, 2003, 2009 by Holman Bible Publishers. Used by permission. HCSB® is a federally registered trademark of Holman Bible Publishers.

Scripture quotations marked NIV have been taken from The Holy Bible, New International Version® NIV®. Copyright © 1973 1978 1984 2011 by Biblica, Inc. TM. Used by permission. All rights reserved worldwide.

Scripture quotations marked NLT are taken from the *Holy Bible,* New Living Translation, copyright © 1996, 2004, 2007, 2015 by Tyndale House Foundation. Used by permission of Tyndale House Publishers, Inc., Carol Stream, Illinois 60188. All rights reserved.

ISBN: 978-1-700-15744-7

Dedication

This devotional is dedicated to my sorority sisters and my sisters in Christ. I have devoted this to my sorority sisters because I want them to always be reminded of who they are, where they came from, and who they hope to be. They may not realize it, but they helped shape me, and I want to help shape them in Christ as well. And for all girls out there, this is for you. This is for you because you should never have to go a day without knowing Who's you are, where your beauty comes from, and how loved you are. Regardless of what the world says, sisters, you are all beautiful. Every single one of you. No matter your mistakes or flaws. You are the beautiful daughter of the Lord Jesus Christ. Never forget it.

With Thanks To

Many people helped with the creation of this devotional—from the very first steps to the last one. First off, I would like to thank an old friend, Ethan, for giving me the idea to explore what inner Godly Make Up should be. Thank you to everyone who helped me work through and edit my ideas including Marissa Olson and Dr. Amy Wintermantel. Additionally, I would like to thank Dr. Danielle Hemingson, the faculty sponsor of my research survey titled "College-Aged Women's Views of Themselves." Thanks also to the very talented and creative Erynne Jamison. Thank you for combing so carefully through this devotional as the final editor and cover artist. I owe the final product to you. For my family and friends: thank you for being the encouragement I needed as I wrote and published this devotional. Finally, and always most importantly, thanks be to God. These words are not truly my words, but His words. I only hope that with every word I wrote, I am speaking His truths for the world to hear and thus, fulfilling the purpose He has given me.

Introduction

When I woke up this morning, I washed my face and then slapped on some foundation and mascara before I finished getting ready and went out to brunch. But why did I feel like I had to do that? Why did I think that I needed to cover up or hide the blemishes on my face with makeup just to go eat some lemon ricotta pancakes? Because according to our culture, makeup makes us beautiful. According to an article posted to Mint.com, four in five women wear makeup, the average woman spends $15,000 on makeup in her lifetime, and on average, women spend twenty minutes putting on makeup each day—that's more than 121 hours per year![1] With all this power and weight given to makeup and our outward beauty, it's no wonder that many girls and women have low self-esteem. Self-image determines our beauty and our worth, or so society says.

But the truth is that what the world says is vastly different than what God says. To God, you are not just the makeup you wear or the name brand clothes you own. The Creator of this Earth also created you, and He thinks that you are His unique, beautiful, and valuable daughter. He loves you so much that He gave His only son to die for you—to save you from your sins and to make you an heir in heaven. Despite your inner and outer flaws, you are chosen by God, your sins are forgiven the moment you ask for forgiveness, and you have a new name and a new identity.

Makeup no longer defines your beauty, instead your Godly Make Up does. Your Godly Make Up is what you're made of—the fruit of the Spirit, the truth of God, the perfectly imperfect quirks that make you the only you there is. You may put makeup on your face to cover your blemishes, but your Godly Make Up should not be hidden. Expressing your Make Up shares your character, faith, and most importantly, your God to the world. You may not know exactly who God calls you to be or who God says you are, and that's why I wrote this devotional. I hope that my words share with you that God says your beauty shines through your Godly character and that you do not need makeup to hide yourself. You are God's child, so you are perfectly made—you do not need makeup to prove that.

Each day in this one-month devotional is broken up into four parts. First there is the *foundation*, which is the day's Bible verse that lays the foundation for the rest of the day much like cosmetic foundation prepares your face for the rest of your makeup. The essential verse that is the cornerstone for our entire journey is 1 Peter 3:3-4. This verse says, "Your beauty should not come from outward adornment, such as elaborate hairstyles and the wearing of gold jewelry or fine clothes. Rather, it should be that of your inner self, the unfading beauty of a gentle and quiet spirit, which is of great worth in God's sight."[2] This verse tells us all we need to know about our Make Up—that it has everything to do with our inner-selves and not our outward appearances.

Next, each day will break down the foundational Bible verses and answering the essential questions. This is the powder. The essential questions for this devotional are:

- What do you, others, and most importantly, God, say about your Make Up?
- What is your Godly Make Up, and how can you deepen that Make Up so that the young woman you were created to be shares God's love to the world?
- What does God say about you, and how can your Make Up support what God says about you?

As I explain these questions through anecdotes, explaining the Bible verses, and research from the survey I conducted on my college-campus,[3] I hope you begin to understand the answer to them. It might even be helpful to keep a journal, so that throughout your journey you can write what you learn about yourself, God, and your Make Up.

Each day will also have an essential point, or the mascara. Mascara is my favorite cosmetic item because I feel like it really brightens my eyes and helps them stand out. The black thick lines of mascara make a statement. That's why I decided that the essential point, or the most important part to take away from each day, is the mascara of our devotional. This essential point, when learned, will help highlight your Godly character in a bold way.

Lastly, just to expand on our Bible learning and essential questions, each day will have an extension activity, which I call the lipstick. I don't always wear lipstick, but when I do, people notice. Why? Because something is different about me. If you put the extension activity and your new understanding of your Godly Make Up into practice, then you will become a changed person. God will transform your thoughts and habits, and most importantly, your heart so that it looks more like His. I encourage you to take the few extra minutes to complete the extension activity every day, and see if, like lipstick, others will notice.

I want to end this introduction with the essential point to our entire journey: Your beauty comes from God and only God, and thus, your job is to shine your inner, God-given beauty through your Godly Make Up so others can see Him in and through you.

And with that, it's time for a makeover.

-Hannah

Day 1: God's Daughter

Foundation:

"But to all who believed Him and accepted Him, He gave the right to become children of God." ~John 1:12 (NLT)

"'Because he[a] loves me,' says the Lord, 'I will rescue him; I will protect him, for he acknowledges my name.'" ~Psalm 91:14 (NIV)

Powder:

When I was little, I had this green shirt that read in sparkly pink letters, "Yes, I am a princess. My Father is the King of Kings." I mean, what little girl doesn't want to be a princess, but the best part is that God is my heavenly Father. My earthly dad sets a high standard by always comforting me and making me laugh. He is a great example of who God is and what His heart stands for by teaching me about the Lord and by loving me endlessly. But girl, no one knows how to love us better than our heavenly Father.

The first verse above says that we can become children of God if we only *believe* in Him. Regardless of who your earthly parents are, or who you are, He can still redeem us and make us His children. Not only that, but we can be heirs to the kingdom of God. Both verses tell us how we can become children of God. First, you have to believe in and accept God as your Savior, then you have to love the Lord by acknowledging His name and confessing your sins to Him.

Because you are God's daughter, you have a heavenly Father, who will give you a home and His inheritance. Be confident and unafraid because God is always protecting you. Lastly, know that you are God's servant to lead our lost prodigal brothers and sisters to Him. Because the truth is, the survey I conducted on my college campus showed me that for as many women who say they are God's daughter currently, there is an equal number of women who do not feel that way yet[3]. Let's rejoice that we know the kingdom and crown we have inherited, but let's also help spread the kingdom to other women so we can all be princesses of the King.

Mascara:

When you accept God, He becomes your heavenly Father and you, his daughter.

Lipstick:

Draw or make yourself a crown (hey look, there's one in the index[4]) to remind you, for the rest of this journey, that your Make Up is being God's daughter. If it would help you, write today's verse or the phrase I shared on it. You are a princess, so don't think of yourself as any less.

1

Day 2: Forgiven

Foundation:

"'Come now, let us settle the matter,' says the Lord. 'Though your sins are like scarlet, they shall be as white as snow; though they are red as crimson, they shall be like wool.'" ~Isaiah 1:18 (NIV)

"If we confess our sins, he is faithful and just and will forgive us our sins and purify us from all unrighteousness." ~1 John 1:9 (NIV)

Powder:

When *God* says that we are going to settle the matter of our sin, the Lord of Lords is proving to you once and for all that you are forgiven. No ifs, ands, or buts about it, the truth is that you are forgiven. However, to be forgiven must mean that you were a sinner to begin with. You have to own your sin and confess to God, knowing you are a sinner, so He will forgive you. Your sins are red, yet they have been wiped clean as snow; your debt has been paid.

As a child of God, you are His sheep. He is your shepherd and He will do everything to keep you safe and clean. Running around in the world, your wool will get dirty from getting cuts and bruises. Jesus will rescue you and save you, cleaning up your cuts and letting you start over. You will no longer roam out in the wilderness, dirty and alone. God is right there calling you back saying, "Daughter, you can run home to me. Always. No sin can keep you away from me. I will always forgive you and make you clean."

If God says all these things about you, then you have to do something about it. You are forgiven for any sin you commit, but you should not sin whenever you want. You can't take life for granted, so live life the way God asks you to. Follow Him, obey his commandments, be kind to your neighbors, lend to the poor and underprivileged, and spread the Word with those who don't know Christ. Let your inward personality and outward appearance reflect a person who is forgiven by a gracious God and wants to please Him as much as she can.

Mascara:

You are forgiven. Period. End of story.

Lipstick:

On the inside of your palm, write sinner in red washable marker. Throughout the day, each and every time you wash your hands, watch the word disappear just like it did when God forgave you and made you white as snow.

Day 3: Chosen

Foundation:

"For you are a people holy to the Lord your God. Out of all the peoples on the face of the earth, the Lord has chosen you to be his treasured possession."
~Deuteronomy 14:2 (NIV)

Powder:

It can be hard to believe that God chose you to be His daughter. In fact, only 0.5 percent of the people who participated in my survey said they felt chosen was a quality that described them[3]. Even though it is hard to understand how and why God chose us to be his children (because let's face it, I'm me and you're you), He did, and He will over and over again. Even on my worst days, God chooses me. When I am running late and have to throw my hair into a ponytail, when I'm driving to work to realize that I accidentally forgot to put on makeup, or when I stayed up until way past my bedtime and have bags under my eyes, even then God still chooses me. When I say something behind a friend's back, am rude to my siblings, or get jealous of my classmates, God still chooses me. No matter what I do or say, God chooses me and gives me a purpose.

And listen—He does the same for you. You are not lost, discarded, or underappreciated by God. You are chosen by God who wants you and believes that you are a prized possession. So what? You have a purpose. When you hear God calling you, listen and fulfill your purpose to honor God and uplift His kingdom. For example, my calling is to teach English and to write devotionals—like the very one you're reading! I am pursuing that purpose until I fulfill it and God calls me to a new purpose. You can have confidence in your identity because the Creator of the earth thinks you are worthy and special. You do not have to impress others because He already picked you. Finally, you have to choose God back. Thank Him for always pursuing you and for choosing you. Love Him the way He loves you—with everything He has.

Mascara:

God chose you and gave you a purpose. Go fulfill it.

Lipstick:

Search for scripture related to spiritual gifts and having a purpose. You can start with some of these: Romans 12, 1 Peter 4:1-11, Ephesians 4, and 1 Corinthians 12. With what you learn, consider or journal about what spiritual gifts God may have given you. God chose you and gave you a purpose.

Day 4: Loved

Foundation:

"For God so loved the world that he gave his one and only Son, that whoever believes in him shall not perish but have eternal life." ~John 3:16 (NIV)

Powder:

YOU ARE LOVED!!! Excuse me for yelling at you, but according to my campus survey, only five percent of women feel loved right now[3], and I want to be loud enough so the other ninety-five percent can hear me! Knowing that you are God's child who is forgiven and has a purpose is essential, but if those things are true (which they are), then you should know that you are loved. Because you are loved, you can know that everything else about your identity is true as well—you are beautiful, priceless, and strong. Whether or not you have a significant other or you have hundreds of followers on Instagram, you are loved by God.

Being loved is not a quality that can be hidden. Because God cares about you, you should care about yourself. Do not self-harm or criticize yourself because the Creator of the Universe created you and loves His creation. Believe God's words are true and take care of yourself because here's the thing: you never have to *earn* God's love, but you do have to *accept* it, *believe* it, and *show* it. When you believe you are loved, you can shine that truth and help others believe that they are also loved. Maybe other people need someone to yell the truth at them (kindly, of course). Maybe other people need to be told that God loves them so much that He sent his own son to die for their salvation.

So, sister, here's me telling you so that you can tell others: You. Are. Loved. There's nothing that you can ever do that would change God's mind about you. He loves every little thing about you. Even on your worst days, when you feel unlovable, when you feel like God is going to give up on you, He is right there with you, arms open wide, whispering (or yelling) in your ear, "You are loved."

Mascara:

Even if you do not feel loved by the world, you are loved unconditionally by the Lord.

Lipstick:

Find a piece of paper, preferably red or pink, cut out a heart, then write, "I am loved" on it. Write the Bible verse on the back. Then, put it by your bed so that you can read it and be reminded every single morning and night. There's no better way to start or end your day :)

Day 5: Free

Foundation:

"But now that you have been set free from sin and have become slaves of God, the benefit you reap leads to holiness, and the result is eternal life." ~ Romans 6:22 (NIV)

Powder:

In the movie, *God's Not Dead,* the elderly woman, despite her dementia and inability to remember her own kids, has faith in God. Her son, however, does not. The old woman shares a very important truth with him although she can't even call him by name and despite his rejection of faith. Although he might be a stranger to her, that does not keep her from telling him that before you accept Christ, you are a slave in a prison, except in this prison the door is wide open, and you have a way out. What an important message for her son to hear.

Sin enslaves, but escape is easy. It's right there in front of us—the way to break your chains is to surrender life to God. When you accept Christ, your sins have no hold on you anymore and you are set free. I have to be honest—you might still feel the pull of your sins trying to entrap you, but ultimately, God's love and power have a stronger pull and they pull you to freedom, if you choose them. God will never force you to accept His freedom, but if accepted, His freedom will never allow you to be enslaved again.

Instead of sin and the devil ruling your heart, God does. You are free from the sins that tangle you in unhealthy relationships, financial issues, jealous thoughts, substance abuse, job dissatisfaction, etc. You are no longer a slave to any of these things; instead, you are a servant of God. But, being God's servant isn't really being a slave at all. You do not have to earn the freedom He offers. You simply have to worship Him, devote yourself to Him, and accept the eternal life that he offers. What a punishment, huh?

Mascara:

Your sin used to trap you in a jail cell, but God paid your bail. Run freely towards Him and away from your sins.

Lipstick:

Search the song "I Am Free" by the Newsboys on YouTube and let it remind you about the freedom you have in Jesus. If you're feeling really fun, find one of the dance motion videos to dance along too.

Day 6: Saved

"If you declare with your mouth, "Jesus is Lord," and believe in your heart that God raised him from the dead, you will be saved. For it is with your heart that you believe and are justified, and it is with your mouth that you profess your faith and are saved." ~ Romans 10:9-10 (NIV)

Powder:

There are many people who make a living by saving—policemen and women, lifeguards, and even goalies. And guess what? You are alive because someone made a save for you. You have been saved by Christ Jesus. About four thousand years ago when He died on the cross for us, our sins were paid for and now we are forever saved. We have life because he died for us and saved us from our sins. Imagine, you were being sentenced to death in prison with a debt you could never pay, but God bailed you out and cleared your slate.

But while this is free for you, it wasn't free for Him. However, being the gracious God that He is, He will not force salvation on you, despite what it cost Him and His son. So, then, here's the catch: you have to sing your ABCs to accept Christ and your salvation—your Christ follower ABC's, that is. First, Admit that you are a sinner and need God's salvation. Then, Believe that Jesus is God's son and has the power to give you salvation. Finally, Confess your faith in Jesus. If you do those things, then Jesus will be your Lord forever and will build a room for you in his heavenly home.

Now, you're probably thinking that this all sounds a lot like what I said about you being free. The truth is, they are very similar because both come from the crucifixion of Jesus as a sacrifice for your sins. They are different because being free results in no longer being chained by sin while being saved means you were rescued from your sins. You are not who you used to be; you are new because God is the life raft that pulled you out of the sea you were drowning in. God is the ultimate Savior for anyone who accepts Him.

Mascara:

Jesus made the greatest save of all time, with His arms stretched wide on a cross. We are saved from our sins, so proclaim your faith and accept your new life.

Lipstick:

What is your salvation story? Maybe write it down so that you can remember the special moment and share it with others.

Day 7: Honest

Foundation:

"Therefore each of you must put off falsehood and speak truthfully to your neighbor, for we are all members of one body." ~ Ephesians 4:25 (NIV)

Powder:

In a world filled with dishonesty and lies, God asks you to be honest and truthful. He sets the perfect example of what honesty looks like because everything He says about you, about the earth, about heaven—it's all true. God comes through on His promises for us every time to prove that He means what He says. Truth is important to God because truth builds trust. We can trust a God who never lies, never changes His mind, and always comes through on His word. You can depend on God.

A hopeful truth that my survey revealed is that young women do feel like they are honest[3]. Seven percent of women said they are honest right now, while five percent of women wanted to practice honesty. I love that women try to be honest, but I also feel like saying we are this honest might be dishonest. The truth is, when is the last time you gossiped with friends? That's not being honest or graceful with your words. Or have you ever told yourself that you aren't good enough, can't do it, won't get the job that you want, or any other lie? That's not honesty, that's listening to the lies that Satan is feeding you. So maybe, the truth is that honesty is hard in a world that teaches us to point out the flaws in ourselves and others. However, the greatest truth that I know is that God loves you, chooses you, and created you. When you choose to be truthful regarding your Make-Up, you directly contradict the dishonesty of Satan. Choose God's truth and the devil will flee. Stop spreading lies about others and instead, build trust with others, create lasting bonds, and shape God's character within yourself. Be an example to the world of what it looks like when you allow God to define your life and live out those truths, rather than letting the devil spread lies into the world.

Mascara:

Being honest with your words and actions is important because it builds trust between you and others, improves your likeness to Christ, and spreads love not lies.

Lipstick:

Identify the area in your life that is filled with the most dishonesty. Are you dishonest with yourself, your parents, your friends? Ask God to give you freedom from the devil's dishonesty and to help you cultivate honesty in that area of your life.

Day 8: Thankful

Foundation:

"Therefore, since we are receiving a kingdom that cannot be shaken, let us be thankful, and so worship God acceptably with reverence and awe." ~ Hebrews 12:28 (NIV)

Powder:

The greatest story of Thanksgiving in American history is of course the story of the Native Americans and the colonists. Even though these two groups also quarreled and endured many illnesses, this first Thanksgiving brought together the two peoples in a peaceful gathering that we still celebrate today. The traditions of the holiday have changed throughout time, yet I think one thing remains true— Thanksgiving is a reminder of what we can be thankful for. As believers—the greatest thing we have to be thankful for is Jesus. Thus, the greatest story of gratefulness is not the one between the Indians and the Europeans but between you and Jesus.

Every day, you have the opportunity to be thankful and show your gratitude to God. You can be thankful for your salvation, the Lord's mercy, and the hope you have in the Lord, You can thank Him for everything He has given you from the sunshine to the shoes on your feet, and for the people He surrounds you with. As the verse says above, "we have received a holy nation that cannot be moved," meaning that what God has given us cannot be taken away. The eternal life promised for us is ours to keep, so friends, let's rejoice and be thankful!

As you worship and thank God, praise Him with other believers as well. Having accountability like this can help you during your hard times when grumbling is easy and gratefulness is hard. Then, do not forget to thank God for your fellow believers. Writing this right now, I know that I would not have made it through this semester without the help of friends and family; I am so grateful for them! Even if you sometimes quarrel with the people in your life, spend time honoring and thanking those people, just like the Native Americans and colonists did way back in 1621.

Mascara:

Today you woke up and had breath flowing in your lungs. You are God's child and have eternal life. Be thankful.

Lipstick:

Write a gratitude list in your journal. It doesn't have to be really long, but as you list anything and everything that you are thankful for, remember that it all comes from God. Check out the link I've put in the index[5] to see some of the proven benefits of gratitude.

Day 9: Perseverance

Foundation:

"Dear brothers and sisters, [a] when troubles of any kind come your way, consider it an opportunity for great joy. For you know that when your faith is tested, your endurance has a chance to grow. So let it grow, for when your endurance is fully developed, you will be perfect and complete, needing nothing." ~ James 1:2-4 (NLT)

Powder:

Every time I sit down to write another ten-page paper for one of my classes, I dread it. I like writing, but completing academic papers takes hours of finding research, writing, and revising. It's not what I would call a fun time, but the more papers I write, the easier it is. I am able to pick a better topic, select better quotes, write the pages faster, and have less to edit. I grow stronger and more determined, my skill set improves, and I become a better writer.

The same happens with our faith when we experience trials. No one likes to be put through trials or hard times, but you can't deny that when you are, you build strength. James 1 tells us that we will be tested but that trials of faith build perseverance of faith. I can guarantee that you will face mountains, maybe today or maybe tomorrow, but those mountains will make you stronger overall, if you let your endurance grow. Growth in this way can be painful, but James 1 says it makes us complete and is a reason for joy.

I can't say how you might be tested. I've fought little battles, like when work is hard, I have a really busy day, or when I have arguments with my loved ones, and I've also fought big battles, like when my dad was in Iraq or when I battled extreme anxiety. Two truths that I remember during my trials are that God only tests me if He knows I can handle it and that He never leaves me on my own in my struggles. Even when I don't feel strong enough, I know I can make my way through the trial because God is on my side and will give me the strength I need. He'll be there with you, too. Rely on Him to help you through your trials and accept the growing pains, knowing they build your endurance.

Mascara:

Even in the worst of trials, God is with you, building your perseverance and your Make Up.

Lipstick:

Meditate on a challenge you are facing right now. Christian meditation relies on lifting your burdens to God and then asking Him to refill you. A great way to do this is to read God's word and reflect on how it applies to your current trial and the deliverance God will bring to it.

Day 10: A Holy Temple

Foundation:

"For we are co-workers in God's service; you are God's field, God's building...Don't you know that you yourselves are God's temple and that God's Spirit dwells in your midst? If anyone destroys God's temple, God will destroy that person; for God's temple is sacred, and you together are that temple." ~1 Corinthians 3:9, 16-17 (NIV)

Powder:

You know how everyone always says that the inside is more important than the outside, but that you never really believe them because how can that be true if the first thing people see is not your heart but your body? How is that true when society places so much value on photoshopped Instagram photos? Well, for Christians, it is true and very important because the Holy Spirit lives in us. It is not about what our outside looks like but what our hearts look like because the Spirit lives in us and because our hearts reflect the image and love of Jesus Christ.

The verses above say that we are God's—we are His coworkers, His field, His building, and His holy temple. As God's coworker, you share in the work of His kingdom; He has a purpose for you. You are also His field, and God grows His character in you. Lastly, you are God's building and holy temple. God lives in you, and your body is sacred to Him. What are you doing to take care of God's sacred home? Do you care for your heart by growing the fruit of the Spirit in you? The greater the presence of God in you, the greater your protection against the devil's snares. Do you look after your soul by recognizing Who lives there? The Holy Spirit guides your soul and acts like a compass. Lastly, how well do you take care of your physical body? To take care of your body, do you eat healthy, exercise, and use positive self-talk?

Doing all these things, and more that you enjoy, can help you to build your holy temple to be worthy of housing the Holy Spirit. But, please, sister always remember this: your self-worth is not determined by the makeup on your face but your Godly Make Up. Choose to serve the Lord by honoring the soul, body, and heart He gave you.

Mascara:

Honor God by honoring His holy spirit who lives in you and by taking care of your holy temple.

Lipstick:

Go on a walk or eat a really healthy meal today to honor the holy temple that God has given you and that He has chosen to reside in.

Day 11: Humble

Foundation:

"In the same way, you who are younger must accept the authority of the elders. And all of you, dress yourselves in humility as you relate to one another, for 'God opposes the proud but gives grace to the humble.' So humble yourselves under the mighty power of God, and at the right time he will lift you up in honor." ~1 Peter 5:5-6 (NLT)

Powder:

C.S. Lewis states, "True humility is not thinking less of yourself; it is thinking of yourself less." Being humble is not about putting yourself down, it is about lifting others up. It is about letting your heart and mind be consumed with helping others rather than thinking of yourself or how many likes you have on Instagram. No matter how much our human tendency is to pay attention to ourselves, instead we should humble ourselves and focus on others like Jesus did. Being humble is "having or showing a modest or low estimate of one's own importance" and instead uplifting the importance of others (Dictionary.com).

I have divided the people that we need to be humble around into three categories (hint: if you add all the categories together, they equal everyone). The first person we need to approach in humility is God. God asks us to be humble and put him first, to make that part of our identity. You can show that you are a servant of God by letting Him be Lord over your life, thanking Him for how He's blessed you, and give glory to Him for your successes.

It is also important to humble yourself under authorities and elders. I know this is hard because your parents can seem so controlling or because you don't agree with whoever is in office right now. Despite this, God has given these people power so humble yourselves under them by honoring, obeying, and respecting them even if you disagree with them. This leads into the last category—everyone else. The greatest way to humble other people is to put them first. Show them that you do not think of yourself as better than them but rather that you are there to support, encourage, and serve them. If you humble yourself in these ways, others will notice your kind servant leadership, you will be easier to work with, and you will please God.

Mascara:

Being humble means thinking of yourself less so that you can put others first.

Lipstick:

Whether you serve others first at dinner, let someone go in front of you in line at Walmart, or pray for other's needs, try to think of yourself less and others more today.

Day 12: Generous

Foundation:

"Whoever is kind to the poor lends to the Lord, and he will reward them for what they have done." ~Proverbs 19:17 (NIV)

Powder:

In the Bible, several groups of people are listed that we should center our focus and generosity towards. Those groups are widows, orphans, and the poor or marginalized. To God, these groups need our help, so He calls us to lend to and help them without asking for anything in return. The verse above focuses on being kind to the poor, but the point is the same: if you help others, you are working for God's kingdom. God by no means needs your help or your donations, but He wants someone to work through. If He is calling on you to donate your clothes to the local Salvation Army, to serve at your community soup kitchen, to spread awareness about healthy relationships, or to financially adopt an orphan from Thailand, then do it. Show up for others that need your help in the best way that you can.

God doesn't often promise reward, but when He does, you can be sure that it is something that is really important to Him. I cannot promise you that you will be rewarded in this life, but I know you will be rewarded with eternal life. Each time you help others, God is saying, "Well done, daughter" and is waiting to welcome you home in heaven with gifts, jewels, and a room in His house. Your reward will be tenfold what you ever give, so if God is asking you to be generous, obey Him and trust that if He asks you to give to meet other's needs, He will provide for your needs as well. More importantly, don't be generous just because you want to be rewarded—be generous because God is. He gave himself (God and Jesus are one and the same!) for you! He calls for you to be generous because generosity is a part of his Make Up and thus, should be a part of yours if you are to be like Him.

Mascara:

Being generous to widows, orphans, the poor, and the marginalized is doing work for God's kingdom, and those who work for Him will be rewarded with eternal life.

Lipstick:

For the remainder of this devotional, collect the change that you get back from any purchases. At the end, donate all the money to your favorite nonprofit or add it to your tithe for your church.

Day 13: Grace

Foundation:

"But he said to me, 'My grace is sufficient for you, for my power is made perfect in weakness.' Therefore I will boast all the more gladly about my weaknesses, so that Christ's power may rest on me." ~2 Corinthians 12:9 (NIV)

Powder:

Grace, according to my campus research study, is a quality that young women feel that they do not currently possess and do not think they will possess in the future[3]. Yet, I believe that as women we are called to be graceful because we have been given grace. In fact, we have been given grace like Mary Poppin's bag—every time you reach in for more, thinking that surely you have reached the bottom of the bag, there is still grace spilling out for you.

We get to heaven because of God's grace and then, His grace fuels everything we do. You can never use it all up because God's grace never runs out and is more than enough. When we have weaknesses or faults, the Lord's power swoops in and gives us grace. Grace is forgiveness even when we don't deserve it and a one hundredth chance even though we shouldn't even get a second. And, God's favor is free! God will freely give you His grace if only you would ask for it and honor Him with your thanks and worship.

Wearing God's grace looks like walking in obedience, asking for forgiveness when you mess up, being thankful for your salvation, trusting in God's power, and not being afraid to make mistakes. Wearing grace is important because if you can realize that the bag of grace is never empty, but always completely full for you, then you can give out FULL grace to others too. The more you realize that you have been given abundant grace, pass it on to others. Be graceful to others: forgive their faults, leave room for mistakes, give freely, be slow to anger, and be quick to show kindness.

Mascara:

God's grace for you is bottomless, just like Mary Poppin's bag.

Lipstick:

Listen to the song "Grace Wins" by Matthew West. Matthew and his dad, who is a pastor, wrote the song about a young man who was addicted to heroin but knew he wanted to be a child of God and be redeemed. They spoke with the man about accepting Christ and the grace He offers. Your story of grace is likely very different, but the truth is still the same—God's grace wins and saves you.

Day 14: Hope

Foundation:

"I pray that God, the source of hope, will fill you completely with joy and peace because you trust in him. Then you will overflow with confident hope through the power of the Holy Spirit." ~Romans 15:13 (NLT)

Powder:

If you watch or listen to the news for even just a few minutes, it can be hard to have hope for this world. As Luke Bryan would say, "I believe if you just go by the nightly news, your faith in all mankind would be the first thing you lose" ("Most People Are Good"). A few weeks ago, I was watching the news and heard that one of my neighbors, who was a police officer, was killed on duty. And then, there was a bombing in Paris. Or the construction worker who went off one day at work and pulled out a gun. There's just a whole lot of destruction and sadness that makes it hard to believe in something better.

The good thing is that we don't have to get our hope from this world because, let's be honest, it wouldn't deliver. When we get our hope from God, we then have the opportunity for hope to be a part of our Make Up. Sadness defines the world, and even as believers, we will have times of sorrow. However, we also have the promise from Christ that joy comes in the morning and thus, we can have hope even in our sadness. When you have hope, you will have joy and peace because of your trust. Hope takes trust in the God who holds your future. Trust that He will provide and that He has a brilliant plan for you. Then, you can have hope, joy, and peace and look forward to your future.

The verse above also tells us that we will have *confident* hope. Hope has an amount of certainty to it. For example, I hope I have three kids someday, but the future is pretty uncertain. I do not know what my far future looks like or how many children God wants to grant me with. Yet, God says He has plans to prosper me, to give me hope and a future (Jeremiah 29:11). Thus, I can be hopeful towards the future God has planned for me, even if I do not know the details, because I am confident in God's word and His promises.

Mascara:

You can have overflowing, confident hope, even in this world, because God is the abundant source of hope.

Lipstick:

Visit the Good News Network website to read about positive news stories happening in our world today. They can remind you that there is hope in this world, and His name is Jesus.

Day 15: Priceless

Foundation:

"A wife of noble character who can find? She is worth far more than rubies."
~Proverbs 31:10 (NIV)

"For you know that it was not with perishable things such as silver or gold that you were redeemed...but with the precious blood of Christ" ~1 Peter 1:18-19 (NIV)

Powder:

Wealth is so valued in this world. People are always trying to earn more money and then spend the money to show others how much money they have: "Why, yes, Hannah, I do have a working 100 inch screen TV at home, but I just got my bonus from work and thought I would spend it right away on a 102 inch screen TV."

Money has always been important and prized in society—including in Bible times. Rubies, especially, were a very valuable gem. To show us how much we mean to Him, God compared us to rubies, knowing how precious rubies were to people. In fact, God spent something even more valuable than rubies to save us—His son's precious blood. To Him, you are not only more precious than rubies, but you are also worth the blood of His son shed on the cross. Up on the cross, Jesus was in pain, so much so that he sweat blood. Yet, if you would ask Him, He would say it was worth it because it saved you, His precious, precious daughter. To the world, you might not be on a Forbes list or have stacks of cash, but to God, you are priceless.

When thinking about your Make Up, do not forget how valuable, special, and purposeful you are. God gave up everything for you because, to Him, you are worth it. You may have days where your self-esteem starts to decline, but lift it back up with the encouragement that God thinks you are so precious.

Mascara:

Your value comes from God, not the world, and He says that you are more precious than rubies and worth Jesus's blood on the cross.

Lipstick:

Put a dollar on your dash or your refrigerator to remind you that you are worth more than any worldly possession. You are priceless to God!

Day 16: Wonderful

Foundation:

"For you created my inmost being; you knit me together in my mother's womb. I praise you because I am fearfully and wonderfully made; your works are wonderful, I know that full well." ~Psalm 139:13-14 (NIV)

Powder:

Someday down the line I may have a little munchkin stumble up to me and ask, "Mommy, where did I come from?" At some point or another, all kids probably ask their parents that question and receive an answer about the storks dropping him off or God putting her in Mommy's tummy. My kids will be told the former—God made you! This will be my future husband and I's opportunity to tell my kids of their amazing creation and how they're story began in God's hands before Mommy and Daddy even knew they were coming.

I hope you've heard this story before, but in case you haven't or you need a recap, here it is: God made you from the inside out, knitted you in your mother's womb, and created you to look like and strive to be like Him. Now, you may think that God couldn't have created you because you have too many mistakes. Whether they be physical imperfections or character flaws, that's Satan speaking because God does not make mistakes. My wide hips or your tendency to worry are not mistakes, they make us the unique individuals God made us to be. We are perfectly imperfect.

All of God's works, including you, are wonderfully made. You are special and unique. God is the potter, and I am an oddly shaped, hard to work with lump of clay. Still, God did not give up on me. He saw the potential in me to be wonderful and so He molded me to look like Him and continues to mold me so that my heart looks like His. The same is true of you. God created you and continues to shape you so that you can be more like Him. God gave you your abilities, characteristics, and traits, so do not be ashamed of them but recognize that they make you unique and wonderful.

Mascara:

God made you just how He intended, so know that your uniqueness is wonderful!

Lipstick:

Write a positivity list about yourself—do not focus on or even think about the things about you that need improvement. Instead, write what you like about yourself and qualities that make you *you*.

Day 17: Brave

Foundation:

"David replied to the Philistine, 'You come to me with sword, spear, and javelin, but I come to you in the name of the Lord of Heaven's Armies—the God of the armies of Israel, whom you have defied. And everyone assembled here will know that the Lord rescues his people, but not with sword and spear. This is the Lord's battle, and he will give you to us!'" ~1 Samuel 17:45 and 47 (NLT)

Powder:

In the verses above, David was brave not because he was big, strong, or powerful, but because he knows that God is greater than his enemies, God is with him at all times, and that God fights through him. Many of us have heard all about how David killed Goliath with just a stone and went on to fight many armies, but this verse shows that it wasn't David's warrior skills that saved him—it was God. David knew that the God of angel armies was on his side, so he would not need a sword or spear. He put his faith in the Lord and the battle in God's hands. David may have been a teenage boy, but his faith was strong and His God is mighty.

Just like David, every battle we have is not ours to fight alone. We have God on our side to protect us from our enemies, give us strength to keep pushing forward, and to make us brave. When you are in a situation that requires courage, look to the Lord. He will steady your shaking hands and help you to take another step forward.

No matter your battle, whether it be with a school bully, a negative work environment, or with your own fear, it is not too big for God. He will fight your battles alongside you, using His divine power to work all things for your good. God will not fight with aggression, anger, or violence towards the people or things that cause battles in your life. He is a God of love not hate and has the power to fight without swords. Be brave and courageous in the face of fear and danger, but also be kind and compassionate. In this way, you will show the world that your way, and God's way, to fight battles promotes the Lord's love and kingdom and not the devil's violence.

Mascara:

You can be brave and courageous because God fights for and with you.

Lipstick:

Draw a sword on a piece of paper and then write BRAVE inside of it. Put it up somewhere to remind you that your weapon is the bravery God gives you.

Day 18: Beautiful

Foundation:

"You are altogether beautiful, my darling, beautiful in every way.*" ~ Song of Songs 4:7 (NLT)

Powder:

Based off the results of the survey[3], about six percent of women wish to be beautiful but do not currently feel that way. This breaks my heart because the truth is that not only are you beautiful, but EVERY part of you is beautiful! The verse above says in every single way you are beautiful. Now, the verse above is one lover speaking to another, but I believe that God talks about you in this way too! He adores every single thing about you! This is significant because it means that even if you nitpick something about yourself or others criticize you, you're still beautiful. There are no ands, ifs, or buts about it—you are special and you are beautiful.

Believing you are beautiful and raising your self-esteem takes time and hard work. It takes fighting back against the lies about your body. Lies that push you closer and closer to an eating disorder when the truth is that God created you to be healthy, not a size zero. It takes being comfortable in your own skin even if it refuses to do anything but freckle in the summer. It takes being modest, in your clothing and self-presentation. Believing you are beautiful requires you to ignore the whispers behind your back and instead listen to the whispers of the Holy Spirit. And finally, believing you are beautiful means making others feel beautiful as well.

Oh, how I wish I could look at you right now and tell you how beautiful you are. From the inside out, I see God in you and know that God created a beautiful woman, but sister, please stop hiding your beauty from the world. You do not have to hide behind the (earthly) makeup, frills, or name brand clothes anymore. You do not have to change who you are or hide your uniqueness for others to see how beautiful you are. God is the only one who truly knows how to define beauty because He created everything, and He defines beauty as you and me.

Mascara:

You do not need earthly makeup to be beautiful because being God's beautiful daughter _is_ your Godly Make Up.

Lipstick:

*There are many iterations of this verse. My other favorites are ESV and NIV. For today's next step, pick the version of the verse that is your favorite and then insert your name in for "my darling." Write the personalized verse on a notecard and stick it to your mirror. Now, your mirror will deliver truths instead of lies about your self-worth and beauty.

Day 19: Dignity

Foundation:

"She is clothed with strength and dignity, and she laughs without fear of the future." ~ Proverbs 31:25 (NLT)

Powder:

I'm going to be honest with you girls, this is the last devotional that I wrote for this collection. I kept getting stuck on what dignity means and thus, wasn't sure how to, or if I was qualified to, tell you how to be dignified. And according to my survey, other women are unsure of what it means too because less than a percent of women chose dignified to describe themselves now or in the future[3]. However, I know that God calls us to clothe ourselves in dignity, so it must be important and something that we cannot overlook. So, I trudged on and did some research about the definition of dignity and what it means in the Bible.

According to the Merriam-Webster online dictionary, dignity is "the quality or state of being worthy, honored, or esteemed." To me, this means that dignity is holding yourself to a high standard which earns you respect. From the verse above, I can see how this definition would align with the Bible because following God definitely does mean that we hold ourselves to a higher moral and religious standard—not because being a Christ follower is all about rules, but because it's about building a relationship with Christ and becoming more like Him.

Some practical ways that I think we can clothe ourselves in dignity are about how we carry ourselves whether others are watching or not. For example, if someone says a mean comment to you, dignity is holding your chin high and removing yourself from the situation (Hint: dignity is not saying something mean back). Dignity is also about integrity—about caring about how you act even if no one is watching. So, if you see a piece of trash on the ground, pick it up even if you won't receive recognition, if you are watching a movie by yourself, watch an appropriate one even if no one else knows what you are doing, or if you are writing a paper for class, don't plagiarize. Lastly, be dignified as you build a relationship with Christ, knowing that the ultimate goal of dignity is not to earn recognition but to become more like Him. Hold yourself high and clothe yourself in dignity.

Mascara:

Dignity is holding yourself to the higher standards of God whether or not others are looking.

Lipstick:

Hold yourself to a higher standard in the way you talk to others today—don't react negatively.

Day 20: Strong

Foundation:

"Have I not commanded you? Be strong and courageous. Do not be afraid; do not be discouraged, for the Lord your God will be with you wherever you go." ~ Joshua 1:9 (NIV)

Powder:

Being strong and fearless is for heroes, not for those of us without superpowers, right? Wrong! Strength is a quality that women possess not only because of the way God designed our bodies but also because of how He designed our hearts. God created women with the capability of childbirth, so our bodies contain the strength to grow and carry a human being for nine months. Also, our hearts, as broken as they feel in our pain and suffering, keep beating, proving their resilience. Thus, women are strong. Five percent of the women in my survey said they felt strong and that they wanted to be strong. With today's attention on feminism and gender equality, women are realizing that strength is just as innately a female quality as it is a male.

However, sometimes we act strong on the outside while we are breaking on the inside. I've been told that I am a strong person, yet I feel like I have been knocked down a lot; I don't feel all that strong, but I know that my God is strong. He gets me through when all I want to do is cuddle up into a ball under my covers. The whole time, though, God is right there. He never leaves me in my trials, instead he saves me and surrounds me with His strength and defenses. When you are feeling weak and overwhelmed, God is right there for you too. His strength is more than enough for you, so just ask for it. Ask him to refill your strength when it has run out.

You can have strength in the highs and lows by knowing that God is right beside you. I can't predict what trials may come your way, but I know they will. When they do, you do not have to let them shake you or tear you down because you have God's strength to lift you up. As the quote goes, "life is tough, but so are you." Don't be afraid and know that you are not weak because the God with enough strength to hold together this broken world also holds you.

Mascara:

When you are going through hard times, you can be strong and unafraid because our God of endless strength is with you.

Lipstick:

Journal about an instance when you felt weak and afraid. Then, write about a time that you felt strong and fearless. What would both situations have looked like if more of God was added to each?

Day 21: Wisdom

Foundation:

"She speaks with wisdom, and faithful instruction is on her tongue." ~ Proverbs 31:26 (NIV)

Powder:

Proverbs 31 explains a ton about what it means to be a godly woman (I highly recommend you read it if you haven't). Verse 26 clearly describes how we should speak, and that as a woman, wisdom needs to be a part of our words. Before wisdom can be something that you comfortably share, though, it needs to be in your heart. You can grow wisdom in your heart by reading God's word, and thus learning about Him. The deeper your relationship with Christ, the more wisdom He will share with you.

I've always had trouble feeling like I was wise enough to make the right decisions for my life. It causes me to be very indecisive, but one thing I learned that makes it much easier is that I don't have to depend on my own wisdom. Instead, I can depend on the genius who created the universe and keeps it all in motion the way it should be—God! Unfortunately, even with God's wisdom, decision making is still hard. This is because God's advice doesn't always come as whispers in our ears when we sit and wait for a sign from God. Rather, it comes from spending time with God in prayer, reading your Bible, and asking Him to give you the wisdom to do the right thing. The more time you spend with God, the more you know about Him and the more you understand about his wisdom. This is important because then you will be able to discern the Holy Spirit's voice.

Always remember that true knowledge comes from God and teach yourself to listen to the Holy Spirit in your heart; then, you can speak and act with wisdom. This looks like being someone others go to for advice, not making rash decisions, thinking before speaking, and kindly pointing those who have strayed back to God. A wise woman looks out for herself and for those around her because she has been given the greater understanding of the Lord.

Mascara:

A godly woman has wisdom in her heart so she can speak and act with wisdom.

Lipstick:

Open up your Bible and read about the Lord. It doesn't really matter what part but try to read for at least fifteen minutes. During that time, see what insight and wisdom you can gain about the Lord and the life He wants you to live. (Hint: Proverbs has a LOT to say about how to gain wisdom and live out that wisdom in your life, so it might be the book to start with!)

Day 22: Self-Control

Foundation:

"The acts of the flesh are obvious: sexual immorality, impurity, and debauchery; idolatry and witchcraft; hatred, discord, jealousy, fits of rage, selfish ambition, dissensions, factions, and envy...But the fruit of the Spirit is love, joy, peace, patience, kindness, goodness, faithfulness, gentleness, and self-control...Those who belong to Christ Jesus have crucified the flesh with its passions and desires. Since we live by the Spirit, let us keep in step with the Spirit." ~ Galatians 5:19-25 (NIV)

Powder:

Imagine a kid in a candy store, then imagine an adult in a candy store. What, if anything, would be different in their behavior? What would be similar? Who would exercise more self-control? I would imagine that although the adult would be enticed to buy candy, she would be able to contain her wants, knowing that candy isn't exactly part of a balanced diet and that she doesn't want to spend money today. The kid, though, probably has his fingers all over the candy jars, looks for samples, and begs her mom to buy her some.

The verse above says that our old childish ways have been crucified; the passions and desires of the flesh do not control us anymore. Unlike the kid who follows her desires and chooses unhealthily, we belong to Christ and are called to have self-control. Curbing your earthly desires means not letting them lead your life or influence your decisions. Paul lists some of the fleshly desires in the verses above. To you, those desires might include a want for fame or money, the slice of cake in the fridge, the drink offered to you at a party, or the urge to go too far with your boyfriend. However, Paul gives nine specific hopes for you: the fruit of the Spirit. Paul hopes for you to have God's Make Up, to love others, and to be fruitful and multiply. A person with self-control knows how to distinguish between desires that lead towards sin and temptations versus the desires that lead towards God's hope for you to reflect His image.

Mascara:

Self-control is important as a part of your Make Up because it helps control your "kid" desires and behaviors that previously caused you to sin and separated you from God.

Lipstick:

Identify your "kid" desire and take one step to tackle it. For example, your desire could be to watch Netflix all day, but instead get up and go on a walk because you know it is good for you.

Day 23: Gentleness

Foundation:

"Be wise in the way you act toward outsiders; make the most of every opportunity, Let your conversation be always full of grace, seasoned with salt, so that you may know how to answer everyone." ~Colossians 4:5-6 (NIV)

Powder:

Having a tender and kind way of interacting and speaking with others, as well as yourself, is gentleness. According to the passage, being gentle is synonymous being considerate and respectful to others. We need to be gentle because the way you treat others is how they remember you, and *how they remember you is how they remember God.*

This verse tells us that we should always be full of grace when interacting with others. Grace is favor given that is not deserved. God offers you His saving grace daily, even though you are sinful and do not deserve it. Let's be real—we all are broken people who have fallen short of the glory of God, so we can use a break! We need to be treated gently and offered forgiveness, so we do not break even more! Give that same break to others. Grace also means talking in a gentle manner, with kind words that lift others up despite their flaws. "Seasoned with salt" also refers to the way we talk to and behave around others. Salt has been used as a flavor inducer, a preservative, and a healing mechanism. Your words and actions should add flavor to other people's lives—add the joy and hope of the Lord. Your words and actions should also be a preservative by maintaining relationships through thoughtfulness and forgiveness. Finally, they should be a healer because they mend relationships that are falling apart or can heal a friend's pain through a listening ear and kind heart.

The other thing this verse talks about, and which I purposely saved for last, is how we should make the most out of every moment with others. Although this seems like something we all know, I'm not sure that we live it out. Yet, what would your relationships with your family, significant other, friends, and even strangers look like if you took every opportunity to be gentle and kind to them?

Mascara:

Being gentle is about how you treat others with both your actions and words.

Lipstick:

This is going to be a challenge but try, for the entire day, to have conversation that is "full of grace" and "seasoned with salt."

Day 24: Faithfulness

Foundation:

"Observe what the Lord your God requires: Walk in obedience to him, and keep his decrees and commands, his laws and regulations, as written in the Law of Moses. Do this so that you may prosper in all you do and wherever you go and that the Lord may keep his promise to me: 'If your descendants watch how they live, and if they walk faithfully before me with all their heart and soul, you will never fail to have a successor on the throne of Israel.'" ~1 Kings 2:3-4 (NIV)

Powder:

Have you ever gone rock wall climbing? You're strapped into a harness and rope system and you either have someone holding your rope—called a belayer—or have your rope hooked to something at the bottom, ready to catch you should you fall. When you climb, you have to put faith in the things around you for each and every step. You have to put faith in the rock that your foot will climb on, in the equipment and belayer to catch you, and in yourself since you control your balance and movement. You assume certain things to be true and put faith in them, believing that they will do their job to help you get to the top and not get hurt. Building a relationship with God is similar to rock wall climbing because you have to trust in Him to catch you and keep you safe every step of the way.

When you put faith in God, He will prove to you that He can be trusted. God is faithful to us—he is constant, supportive, reliable, and always follows through with His promises. Because God is so dependable, He has given us the perfect example of what faithfulness looks like. He is faithful to us, so we should be faithful to Him. According to the verse above, being faithful includes being obedient to God and his commands and walking in the direction of the Lord with both your heart and soul. Don't obey God's commands because someone else told you it was the right thing to do. Follow the Lord and His decrees because your heart loves Him; do it because your soul is learning to be like the Spirit living inside you. Your obedience shows that you are taking steps in faith towards God, even if the rocks are slippery and you think you might lose your footing. Remain faithful and obedient, knowing that God—the ultimate belayer—is holding you.

Mascara:

Walking in faith means following the Lord and His decrees with your heart and soul.

Lipstick:

Practice being faithful and obedient to the authorities in your life—no complaining or arguing.

Day 25: Goodness

Foundation:

"And I want women to be modest in their appearance. They should wear decent and appropriate clothing and not draw attention to themselves by the way they fix their hair or by wearing gold or pearls or expensive clothes. For women who claim to be devoted to God should make themselves attractive by the good things they do." ~1 Timothy 2:9-10 (NLT)

Powder:

To the world, goodness might look like being a goody two-shoes, always being happy and never upset, the naivety of a child, the gentle touch of your mother, or the taste of your grandma's chocolate chip cookies. On the other hand, goodness to God is about good works. Although good deeds are not how you get to heaven, they can help show others that you are a new person in Christ. Your good deeds show that you care for God's kingdom and that you are growing the fruit of the spirit.

Instead of making people notice what *you* look like, goodness helps others notice what your *heart* looks like and who it follows and adores. That's why it is important for goodness to be a part of your Make Up—not so others see you but so that they see God. If others see good in you and know that you are a Christian, then they will see God through you and realize that God is also good.

Some ways you can practice goodness in your daily life are opening the door for your classmates, helping the elderly woman carry her groceries to the car, offering your time towards your school's volunteer organization, or tutoring a classmate for free. And sometimes, goodness is taking the extra step beyond the obvious. Maybe, you could babysit for the single mother who sits behind you at church. Take the extra initiative so when she comes home that night, her kids will be in bed and her house will be clean. Be devoted to God and focus your good deeds on the people and things that matter to Him.

Mascara:

Your charitable deeds, not what you wear, help show others who and what you stand for.

Lipstick:

Make a bucket list of good deeds that you would like to do for others in your community. Then, start today by checking one or two things off the list and continue tomorrow until performing good works is part of your daily routine.

Day 26: Kindness

Foundation:

"All bitterness, anger and wrath, and shouting and slander must be removed from you, along with all malice. And be kind and compassionate to one another, forgiving one another, just as God also forgave you in Christ." ~ Ephesians 4:31-32 (HCSB)

Powder:

Have you ever heard of servant leadership? When I was a drum major for my high school marching band, this was a topic that we discussed as a band leadership team. Ever since then, when asked how I would describe a good leader, on scholarship or job applications, I say a good leader is a servant. Servant leadership is when the leader, because of how much she cares about who she is leading, puts the group before herself. The greatest example of this occurs when Jesus washes His disciples' feet, found in John chapter 13. Jesus, the leader of the disciples and the one without sin, sat down and washed feet. He put His friends before himself, choosing to spend his last night with them rather than worrying about his upcoming death. This selflessness epitomizes kindness because kindness also requires putting others before yourself.

In the verse above, bitterness and anger are contrasted with kindness and compassion to illustrate the qualities that you should lean away from in order to be more Christ like. Being bitter towards others is not being kind, nor is harboring anger or malice. Rather, forgiving others with compassion and grace is kindness. Really, it can be boiled down to the golden rule: treat others with compassion because that's how you wish to be treated by God. Imagine if God treated you in the same way that you treated others. Luckily, God chooses to forgive you regardless of your shortcomings, but can't you strive to have that same heart? The heart that is kind and forgiving to others regardless of what they have done for you? God calls us to be kind not only because He is kind to us when we don't deserve it, but also because there is no better way to show others that they are loved and valued than by caring for them. God extends love to everyone, including you, so pass it on.

Mascara:

Kindness is caring for others above yourself and treating them as you wish to be treated.

Lipstick:

Be a servant leader today by performing a Random Act of Kindness for someone else. If you need ideas on what to do, check out the internet to see what others have done.

Day 27: Patient

Foundation:

"Be patient, then, brothers and sisters, until the Lord's coming. See how the farmer waits for the land to yield its valuable crop, patiently waiting for the autumn and spring rains. You too, be patient and stand firm, because the Lord's coming is near." ~ James 5:7-8 (NIV)

Powder:

I'm no farmer, but one thing I do know about farming is that crops do not grow overnight. My dad has a garden in our backyard, but it takes him from the very beginning of spring until the fall to get his fruits and vegetables to grow. He has to turn the soil, plant the seeds, water often, and pick the food once it is ready, all while trying to keep my dogs from uprooting his hard work. After weeks of waiting and working, my dad finally gets to pick the first tomato or cucumber to eat. Like the amount of patience needed to wait for the crops to grow, it also takes a lot of patience to wait for the Lord. In one of my favorite movies, *Facing the Giants*, an old man tells the football coach to be patient by preparing his fields for the rain, or by preparing his players for their future opponents. Those who sit around staring at the sky aren't ready for the rain, but those who prime their fields to receive the rain are prepared. The patient farmer, or believer, does what she can while the Lord gets everything organized and ready up in heaven.

The problem is that the waiting is downright awful. I've heard sermons and read devotionals about having patience in the waiting, but friends, this is one of my biggest struggles. Six percent of the women who participated in my survey agree because they said they hope to be, but are not currently, patient[3]. At our age, there is so much ahead of us that we want to happen now, not later. It's hard to see God's plan and be patient when we want a job, spouse, kid, house, or pet so badly. Although patience is not a natural trait for us, we are called to wait for God's perfect timing. When you feel yourself starting to become impatient, consider asking God to give you patience, journaling, or talking with a trusted friend so that you can remain calm and cool as you shine the patience of the Lord.

Mascara:

Be patient like a farmer—prepare your life crops for the rain.

Lipstick:

My challenge for you today is to be patient in a world where fast pace is the status quo and the farming lifestyle is decreasing in need and popularity. In what areas of your life do you specifically need to be patient? Journal a page or so about your plan to be more patient.

Day 28: Peace

Foundation:

"Let the peace of Christ rule in your hearts, since as members of one body you were called to peace. And be thankful." ~ Colossians 3:15 (NIV)

Powder:

Peace in this world is hard because our society teaches go-go-go rather than sit, rest, and be filled with the Lord's peace. Perhaps this is why under one percent of women who participated in my study felt at peace[3]. And girl, I can understand because I'm not a peaceful person either! I am a tightly wound worry-wort who struggles to maintain peace in her daily chaos. I completely get why peace is hard to find in this world. Yet, the world is not our source of peace. With all the chaos, negativity, and stress in this world, there's nowhere to acquire the amount of peace that we need. Instead, we must find our peace in God, be thankful not resentful, and discover the still in the chaos. If we ask God to help us find peace and keep it in our hearts, then we can use it to keep us calm in the face of conflict, disagreements, stress, or tragic events.

Peace is also hard because the world is full of the opposite of peace and encourages an eye for an eye. However, peace is the olive branch that we reach out to others in compromise. We are called to peace with one another, according to Paul in his letter to the Colossians, because we are all one body. This means that we all should work together to recognize the importance of each part. Rather than causing conflict by pointing out flaws, we should play to each other's strengths, and thus, bring peace to the group. Also, just a side point: peace is extending the olive branch to yourself as well! Don't be your own biggest critic—you are God's creation and can be at peace with the woman God is making you to be. Give yourself the chance to breathe in the busyness and leave room for uncriticized error.

Finally, being peaceful is being thankful. A girl who is thankful for what she has doesn't have a reason to be angry or upset about what she doesn't have. She realizes that peace comes from God, not from things. Therefore, she can have peace regardless of her circumstances.

Mascara:

God calls for peace to be a part of your makeup and gives you His peace to hold onto.

Lipstick:

Practice one method of achieving peace today that you think might help you. You could pray, meditate, read your Bible, listen to calming music, or take a warm bubble bath. And if it works, keep it up and watch peace spread into your life.

Day 29: Joy

Foundation:

"Though you have not seen him, you love him. Though you do not now see him, you believe in him and rejoice with joy that is inexpressible and filled with glory, obtaining the outcome of your faith, the salvation of your souls." ~1 Peter 1:8-9 (ESV)

Powder:

I believe that there are four ways to react to the result of a sports game. If you win, then you are either ecstatic with the result because you played hard and earned it or you could win and be happy but know that you still didn't play your best. On the other hand, if you lose, then you can be extremely disappointed or you can have joy because even though the result was undesirable, you can learn and become better overall. Today let's focus on this last category—the difference between joy and happiness and how you can still be joyful in your situations.

First off, it's important to recognize that joy and happiness are not synonyms. While happiness is temporary or fleeting, joy is permanent and lasting. Whereas happiness is found only in good situations, joy can exist in both positive and negative life experiences. And most importantly, happiness comes from yourself, other people, or earthly motives, but joy comes from God, Heaven, and eternal sources.

Challenging situations expect to drag you down, but joy can surface even in those times. You can be thankful of the growth you make during challenges, positive about the possible outcomes, and reliant on God to have a plan. So, for example, during finals week when you are anything but happy to be taking exams and writing papers, you can still be joyful because you are receiving an education that many others will not. Or, when your siblings push your buttons, I know you aren't necessarily happy with them, but be grateful that God gave you friends and family so that you are never alone. Lastly, in your deepest valley of life, whether that be a death in the family, financial issues, or a heart break, you will not be happy. In fact, you will likely be very sad, but you can still be joyful because you have a God who is greater than this world, has amazing plans for you, and is saving you a place in heaven.

Mascara:

Whether you are happy or sad, choose thankfulness and hope. Choose joy.

Lipstick:

A funny video by John Crist inspired parts of today's devotional. Check out the link in the index[6]. Don't be like the football coach; respond to undesirable situations with joy and thanksgiving.

Day 30: Love

Foundation:

"Dear friends, let us love one another, for love comes from God. Everyone who loves has been born of God and knows God. Whoever does not love does not know God, because God is love. This is how God showed his love among us: He sent his one and only Son into the world that we might live through him. This is love: not that we loved God, but that he loved us and sent his Son as an atoning sacrifice for our sins. Dear friends, since God so loved us, we also ought to love one another. No one has ever seen God; but if we love one another, God lives in us and his love is made complete in us." ~1 John 4:7-12 (NIV)

Powder:

Remember that math equation: if a=b and b=c, then a=c? That's like you, God, and love. Since God is love and you are God's, you are also love. I don't know about you, but that just speaks to me on a mind-blowing level. If you know that truth, then you know all you need to know. But, that's why I saved the best part of your Make Up for last, and so I continue...

God loves this world and shows it to us in the way He artfully created the world, blooms the flowers each spring, provides for our needs, performs miracles daily, gives rest to the exhausted mother of young children, and most importantly, sacrificed His own son to save us. But one of the biggest and coolest parts of your identity in God is that you also have the capacity to love people as God works through you to love His children.

God's love is made complete in you. Based on my survey, ten percent of women believe this to be true—the highest percentage of any quality tested[3]! I hope to see that number grow so our world becomes a more loving place. Be grateful that you are loved by the God of the entire universe because He is proud to be your father! Be honored that He gave you the ultimate task of spreading His love. Do not let others go a day without experiencing what it feels like to be loved fully and completely by the Lord. Let God teach you how to love the unlovable because He's the best at it. Finally, never, ever forget that at the core of your identity you are dearly loved by the God of the universe.

Mascara:

God is love, you are God's, and thus, you are love. Go share God's love with the world!

Lipstick:

You were made from love, to spread love, so who is God calling you to love? Write that person a love note—not in a mushy gushy way, but in a "hey, don't forget: God loves you" kind of way.

Conclusion

Now that we have made our way through our thirty-day makeover, I feel transformed and I hope you do too. I hope you can see how beautiful you are in God's eyes. And now, I believe the world will see your beauty more, too, because you are a woman who's beauty shines from the inside out. You shine the love of God with every step you take, with every smile, with every heart touched. You may not know it, but to others, you are God's representative and ambassador. Your Godly Make Up shows others not only who you are, but also who you are striving to be like. That means that through you, others can experience a little bit of what God's love is like. Granted, you are an imperfect, redeemed sinner who can never offer others what God can, but you can be a vessel that God uses. You can show others what God's love looks like through your kindness, joy, grace, and forgiveness. Your beautiful, Christ like Make Up could bring others to know our Lord.

But here's the thing, sister: as much as I want others to see all of these Christ-like characteristics in you, I also want them for you—so that you can know, without a doubt, *who God says you are and who He wants you to be*. With this makeover, I hope you feel like a new woman, a more Christ-like woman, a *beautiful* woman. There is no one else out there like you and despite your flaws, you are blessed to be a uniquely created woman of God. Of course, I want you to go change the world, but you have to change what's in you first. You have to change the way you think about and view yourself because, the truth is, you can't see others how God sees them until you see how He sees you. Even when you sin and even with your excuses, God did not make a mistake when He made you and He did not make a mistake when He destined you to have a beautiful heart like His.

Let's review our foundational, essential verse for a hot second. 1 Peter 3:3-4 taught us that our beauty does not come from the clothes we wear, the cosmetics we put on our face, or the way we style our hair. Rather, our beauty comes from our inner character—from our hearts. Each day, as we yearn to be more like Christ and continue to give ourselves a makeover, we please God.

Sister, please do not close this book without hearing me, one last time: you are God's, you have a beautiful Godly Make Up, and you are so loved. Regardless of how the world defines you, God has the final say. Day after day *after day,* God picks you, flaws and all, to be His daughter. And that, my friend, is your Make Up.

Index

[1] Source from Introduction:

Crooks, Ross. "Splurge vs. Save: Which Beauty Products are Worth the Extra Cost?" *MintLife Blog.* Mint.com, 11 Apr. 2013. Web. 20 Aug. 2018.

https://blog.mint.com/consumer-iq/splurge-vs-save-which-beauty-products-are-worth-the-extra-cost-0413/

[2] Essential Foundation Verse from Introduction: 1 Peter 3:3-4, see following pages

[3] College-Aged Women's Views of Themselves: Survey and Results: see following pages

[4] Crown for Day 1: see following pages

[5] Website for Day 8:

Morin, Amy. "7 Scientifically Proven Benefits of Gratitude That Will Motivate You to Give Thanks Year-Round." *Forbes.com.* Forbes, 23 Nov. 2014. Web. 4 Sept. 2018.

https://www.forbes.com/sites/amymorin/2014/11/23/7-scientifically-proven-benefits-of-gratitude-that-will-motivate-you-to-give-thanks-year-round/#176b9f36183c

[6] John Crist video for Day 29:

Crist, John. "If Football Coaches Were Honest." *YouTube.* YouTube, 5 Oct. 2017. Web. 26 Sept. 2018.

https://youtu.be/-IMP8l175So

"Your beauty should not come from outward adornment, such as elaborate hairstyles and the wearing of gold jewelry or fine clothes. Rather, it should be that of your inner self, the unfading beauty of a gentle and quiet spirit, which is of great worth in God's sight."
~1 Peter 3:3-4

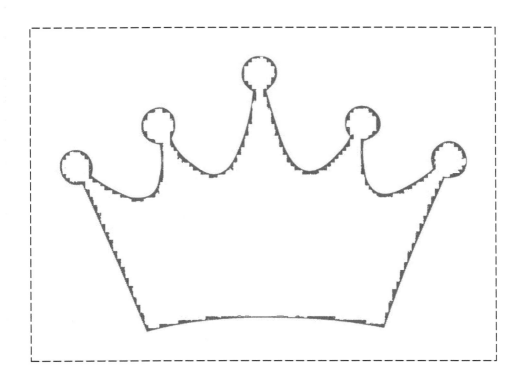

[3]This is an example of the survey I sent out on my campus to gather information for this devotional. I conducted this survey to aid to my devotional by embracing how science and the Bible can work together rather than try to put them at odds with each other.

College-Aged Women's Views of Themselves

My name is Hannah Greer and I will be utilizing this survey to support the devotional that I am writing for my Honors Project. The purpose of this survey is to receive data about how women view themselves. Participation is completely optional—there is not a penalty or a reward for taking this survey. If you should choose to participate, please do not include your personal information on the form at all. Please return your survey to the folder in your chapter house if you live in a sorority or in your RA office if you live in a dorm. The folder will be labelled COMPLETED SURVEYS FOR HANNAH GREER. I will be collecting the folders on Friday, October 26th at 5pm. If you have any questions, comments, or concerns about this survey please feel free to contact me using my campus email, HannahMGreer@stu.bakeru.edu or my faculty advisor at DanielleHemingson@bakeru.edu. Thank you!

1. Circle up to five qualities that you would currently use to describe yourself and/or fill in another option.

Beautiful	Free	Honest	Patient	Valuable
Brave	Generous	Hopeful	Peaceful	Wise
Chosen	Gentle	Humble	Saved	Wonderful
Determined	God's Daughter	Joyful	Self-control	Other:_____
Dignity	Good	Kind	Strong	_____
Faithful	Grace	Loved	A Temple	
Forgiven		Loving	Thankful	

2. Circle up to five qualities that you think you should use to describe yourself (in an ideal world, according to your morals or religion, on your best day).

Beautiful	Forgiven	Grace	Loved	Strong
Brave	Free	Honest	Loving	A Temple
Chosen	Generous	Hopeful	Patient	Thankful
Determined	Gentle	Humble	Peaceful	Valuable
Dignity	God's Daughter	Joyful	Saved	Wise
Faithful	Good	Kind	Self-control	Wonderful
				Other:_____

[3]Below are the results of my survey. In the devotionals, I tried to highlight any significant results from my survey, but you can see additional results below. Please note: I conducted this survey on a small university campus. These results can only speak to my campus but can still aid in demonstration.

Question 1 Qualities	Number of times circled	Percentage	Question 2 Qualities	Number of times circled	Percentage
beautiful	10	2.53%	beautiful	24	6.08%
brave	9	2.28%	brave	21	5.32%
chosen	2	0.51%	chosen	4	1.01%
determined	37	9.37%	determined	13	3.29%
dignity	1	0.25%	dignity	3	0.76%
faithful	16	4.05%	faithful	17	4.30%
forgiven	7	1.77%	forgiven	13	3.29%
free	6	1.52%	free	9	2.28%
generous	19	4.81%	generous	16	4.05%
gentle	7	1.77%	gentle	5	1.27%
God's daughter	18	4.56%	God's daughter	21	5.32%
good	8	2.03%	good	3	0.76%
grace	1	0.25%	grace	5	1.27%
honest	28	7.09%	honest	21	5.32%
hopeful	12	3.04%	hopeful	13	3.29%
humble	16	4.05%	humble	19	4.81%
joyful	12	3.04%	joyful	15	3.80%
kind	24	6.08%	kind	16	4.05%
loved	22	5.57%	loved	15	3.80%
loving	39	9.87%	loving	18	4.56%
patient	18	4.56%	patient	24	6.08%
peaceful	3	0.76%	peaceful	12	3.04%
saved	11	2.78%	saved	6	1.52%
self-control	6	1.52%	self-control	6	1.52%
strong	21	5.32%	strong	20	5.06%
a temple	3	0.76%	a temple	13	3.29%
thankful	18	4.56%	thankful	12	3.04%
valuable	10	2.53%	valuable	19	4.81%
wise	7	1.77%	wise	9	2.28%
wonderful	2	0.51%	wonderful	3	0.76%
other	2	0.51%			
TOTAL	395			395	